IF DINOSAURS WERE ALIVE TODAY

Authors
Dougal Dixon & Dan Green

Consultant
Professor Mike Benton
UNIVERSITY OF BRISTOL

With special thanks to our team of illustrators: Simon Mendez, Leonello Calvetti, Frank DeNota, Andrew Kerr, Peter Scott, Franco Tempesta

Project Editor: Simon Breed
Consultant: Professor Mike Benton, University of Bristol
Designer: Steve West
Cover Designer: Mike Buckley
Cover Illustration: Simon Mendez
Picture Research: Giulia Hetherington, Julia Adams, Jo Hanks, Lizzie Knowles

An Hachette UK Company
www.hachette.co.uk

First published in the USA in 2007 by TickTock, an imprint of Octopus Publishing Group Ltd
Endeavour House
189 Shaftesbury Avenue
London
WC2H 8JY
www.octopusbooks.co.uk
www.octopusbooksusa.com

Copyright © Octopus Publishing Group Ltd 2007, 2013

Distributed in the US by
Hachette Book Group USA
237 Park Avenue
New York NY 10017, USA

Distributed in Canada by
Canadian Manda Group
165 Dufferin Street
Toronto, Ontario, Canada M6K 3H6

ISBN 978-1-84898-742-5

Printed and bound in China

10 9 8 7 6 5 4 3 2 1

BRINGING DINOS BACK TO LIFE

A *Tyrannosaurus rex* crashing through the streets, causing chaos, terror, and destruction... that's what you can see on the cover! Superscary AND exciting, isn't it?

Is *that* what life would be like if we shared our planet with the biggest reptiles that ever existed? Would our lives be frighteningly different, or would we just have to adapt?

For more than two hundred years, dinosaurs have fascinated and excited us. Imagine if we could see these amazing creatures from the past in action, and see what they were really like.

The first people to come up with the ideas about what dinosaurs were like often got it wrong. But if we could touch them, walk among them, we would really know!

How awesome would that be? How terrifying would it be to live alongside these giants and monsters from prehistory? And, importantly, could we control them or would they run free? Think how different our cities and landscapes would look if dinosaurs were roaming wild!

How would the dinosaurs cope? Take the huge-necked and long-tailed plant-eaters, for example - how would these ancient herbivores survive in today's world? Would they even be able to digest today's plants and compete with modern animals? Just imagine an elephant getting tickled by the tail of a towering plant-eating dinosaur! Our much-loved, biggest land animal would look tiny!

4

And what about the massive prehistoric meat-eaters? **Could their hunting styles adapt** to the prey that is available today? Would the fearsome *Tyrannosaurus* be nimble and swift-footed enough to catch an antelope? Could ferocious prehistoric hunters compete with today's fastest predator, the cheetah?

The Age of Dinosaurs lasted for around 160 million years, between the Triassic period – 250 million years ago – and the Cretaceous period, which ended 65 million years ago. Some dinosaurs were **the biggest creatures that have ever walked the land,** but there were also chicken-sized dinos alongside the giants. The skies and seas were filled with **massive flying reptiles and gargantuan ocean-dwelling reptiles. Then... these animals were suddenly gone.**

Scientists still do not know for sure what ended the Age of Dinosaurs; it may well have been the impact of a giant asteroid. The sudden extinction of the dinosaurs made way for a new group of animals – **the warm-blooded mammals.** Eventually, **less than 4 million years ago, humans appeared!**

We may never see the dinosaurs as they were... but we can take what we have discovered from their fossils, compare it with what we know about modern animals, and then create astonishing images showing dinosaurs in the modern world.

You are about to see amazing scenes that show **just what life would be like... If Dinosaurs Were Alive Today!**

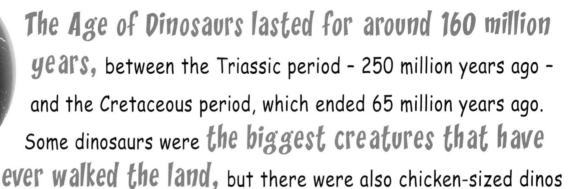

GIANTS OF THE PLAINS

Hey! Watch it, big boy! Under the
African sun, a herd of elephants
gather at a watering hole.
Even though these giant mammals
are twice the height of humans,
they are dwarfed by the greenery-
guzzling monster that lumbers
up behind them!

SAUROPOSEIDON

NAME
Sauroposeidon (say "saw-roe-poss-eye-don") means "lizard of Poseidon" (the earth-quaking Greek God of the Sea).

CLASSIFICATION
Belonged to the titanosaur group of sauropod dinosaurs – the heaviest animals to ever walk the Earth!

TIME
Early Cretaceous period, 112 million years ago.

HABITAT
Open plains with some woodland.

FOSSIL FINDS
Four huge neck bones found in Oklahoma in 1994, and some small fragments in Wyoming. Also footprints and trackways.

Dino Detectives
Paleontologists compared the size and shape of *Sauroposeidon's* neck bones with those of *Brachiosaurus*, and worked out it looked similar – but was much, much bigger. Enormous, in fact!

Sauroposeidon

Brachiosaurus

Elephant

BATTERING RAM

Crack! A bighorn sheep and a Stegoceras slam together in a beserk battle of head-bashing to decide who's boss. This butting contest could last for twenty hours! With its thick skull and strong neck muscles, Stegoceras is one strong dinosaur. The sheep should probably butt out!

STEGOCERAS

NAME
Stegoceras (say "steg-oh-ser-us")
means "roof-horn."

CLASSIFICATION
Belonged to the group of pachycephalosaur
("pack-ee-sef-al-oh-sor") dinosaurs – the
"thick-headed lizards."

TIME
Late Cretaceous period,
77.5-74 million years ago.

HABITAT
Roaming herds, possibly in upland areas.

FOSSIL FINDS
Complete skeletons
from Montana
and Mexico; also
Alberta, Canada.

Bonehead

Stegoceras was a member of the
"thick-headed" dinosaurs. They had a massive
dome of bone on the tops
of their skulls, which
they probably used
to head butt rivals
or foes.

KEEPING COOL

Phew! It's blazing hot, but the Egyptian desert is no sweat for Ouranosaurus. This cool customer controls its body heat with its sail and never gets in a flap!

OURANOSAURUS

NAME
Ouranosaurus (say "oo-ran-oh-saw-rus") means "brave monitor lizard."

CLASSIFICATION
Belonged to the iguanodon ("ig-wah-no-don") group of plant-munching dinosaurs.

TIME
Early Cretaceous period, 110 million years ago.

HABITAT
Tropical lowland forests and swamps.

FOSSIL FINDS
Two (almost) complete skeletons found in Niger, Africa.

Cool Heat Control
As well as using it to cool down, *Ouranosaurus* could use its amazing sail to warm up – in the same way that some lizards flatten their bodies to soak up the Sun's rays.

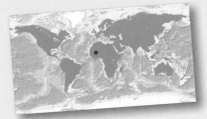

HORNED FACE-OFF

A white rhino holds its ground on the plains of Africa as an angry adult Styracosaurus charges. Pound for pound, these megaheavy horned beasts are evenly matched, but a six-ton pile-up of pure muscle ain't pretty!

STYRACOSAURUS

NAME
Styracosaurus (say "sty-rah-coe-saw-rus")
means "spiked lizard."

CLASSIFICATION
A member of the centrosaur family
of horned dinosaurs.

TIME
Late Cretaceous Period,
76.5–75 million years ago.

HABITAT
Roaming on open plains, sometimes joining
together in large herds.

FOSSIL FINDS
Complete skeletons
from Montana;
also from Alberta,
Canada.

Frilly Frighteners

Styracosaurus's bony
neck frill and nine
horns were a kind of
deadly decoration –
they helped to make it
look like a much bigger
and scarier beast
than it really was.

Triceratops

Styracosaurus

BOXING BuUT

Thwack! Take that, tiger! In a quiet forest glade, a tiger spots lunch, but the young Plateosaurus is not as slow as it looks; a whip of its meaty tail knocks the furry feline off its feet. Outsmarted by a dumb dino!

PLATEOSAURUS

NAME
Plateosaurus (say "plat-ee-oh-saw-rus") means "broad lizard."

CLASSIFICATION
Belonged to the plateosaur family of early dinosaurs.

TIME
Triassic period, 214–204 million years ago.

HABITAT
Low-lying swampy environments.

FOSSIL FINDS
Found across Europe in Germany, France, and Switzerland.

Not-So-Smart Chart

These numbers are a measure of brain size compared to body size. With this score, Plateosaurus is a huge dummy!

Plateosaurus 0.2

Elephant 1.87

Dolphin 5.31

Human 7.44

TAIL DANGER

Three playful lemurs come to take a look at this strange visitor from the past. It's fun to dodge Ankylosaurus's powerful tail club, which – just for a moment – they mistake for its head. Bad mistake!

ANKYLOSAURUS

NAME
Ankylosaurus (say "ang-kai-loh-saw-rus")
means "fused lizard."

CLASSIFICATION
A member of the ankylosaur family of
heavily armored dinosaurs.

TIME
Late Cretaceous period,
66.5–65.5 million years ago.

HABITAT
Warm plains and woodlands, possibly
roaming into upland areas.

FOSSIL FINDS
Many fossil parts
found in Montana
and New Mexico
and in Alberta,
Canada, but no
complete skeleton.

Walking Tank
Ankylosaurus was the biggest
armored dino. Its head was a box
of solid bone, its back was covered in
plates, and it was equipped with a heavy club
at the end of its tail.

AIRPORT INVADERS

A herd of Diplodocus have wandered onto the tarmac. These gigantic dinosaurs are not in the least bit worried by the airplanes. Looks like your flight will be delayed!

DIPLODOCUS

NAME
Diplodocus (say "dip-lod-oh-kus") means "double beam."

CLASSIFICATION
The diplodocid ("dip-lod-oh-sid") family of sauropods were the longest dinosaurs ever.

TIME
Late Jurassic, 154–150 million years ago.

HABITAT
Diplodocus was fond of grazing on trees and shrubs along riverbanks.

FOSSIL FINDS
Many complete skeletons from Colorado, Montana, Utah, and Wyoming.

Long-Legged Lizard

This is how the femur (thigh bone) of *Diplodocus* sizes up against the thigh of a human being like your dad.

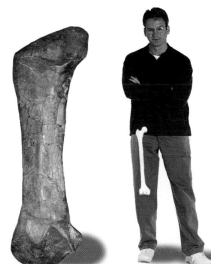

HERD MENTALITY

A pair of sheepdogs keep a herd of Psittacosaurus dinosaurs under control. These shy, plant-eating animals might be farmed for their meat if they lived today. Dino burger, anyone?

PSITTACOSAURUS

NAME
Psittacosaurus (say "sit-uh-ko-saw-rus") means "parrot lizard."

CLASSIFICATION
These parrot-beaked plant-munchers belonged to the ceratopsian dino group.

TIME
Early Cretaceous, 130–100 million years ago.

HABITAT
Scrublands and deserts.

FOSSIL FINDS
Complete skeletons common across Asia – found in Siberia, Russia, Mongolia, and China.

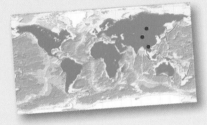

Nip and Bite

Psittacosaurus had a sharp beak shaped like that of a modern parrot. But, unlike a parrot, it also had teeth – for slicing through tough plants and cracking open seeds and nuts.

MILD MONSTER

People at this bustling riverside in South America go calmly about their business as a family of slow-moving Amargasaurus browse the vegetation on the banks. For the kids, these gentle giants are just a part of everyday life.

AMARGASAURUS

NAME
Amargasaurus (say "am-ar-ga-saw-rus") means "lizard of La Amarga."

CLASSIFICATION
These smallish sauropods belonged to the dicraeosaurid ("die-cray-oh-sawr-id") family.

TIME
Early Cretaceous period, 130–125 million years ago.

HABITAT
Along the banks of South American (and possibly South African) rivers.

FOSSIL FINDS
One single, fairly complete specimen found in Argentina.

Spines and Skin

The family of dinosaurs to which *Amargasaurus* belonged had a row of rather fancy spines running down their necks and backs. Scientists think that the ones on the back might have been covered by skin, like those of *Ouranosaurus*.

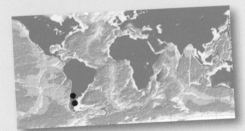

FARM ANIMALS – OR FOREST MUNCHERS?

Giant plant-guzzling dinos blundering about would cause chaos in today's world…

were in dinosaur times – they're mostly found in mountainous areas. If they could stand the cold, long-necked plant-eaters would thrive in these zones.

Dino numbers

There are always more plant-eating animals than meat-eaters. On the plains you might see whole herds of grazing *Diplodocus*.

ARAUCARIA TREE

As with all animals, the plant-eating dinosaurs evolved along with the food that they ate. Short-needled conifers, such as redwoods and cypresses, evolved with the ancestors of sauropods. Dinosaurs such as Diplodocus were perfectly adapted to munching and digesting these tough plants. Today, there are not as many conifers as there

DINO THEME PARK

We love to see big animals up close, but would it be practical to keep such big animals in a zoo or safari park? If we were to keep herbivores in captivity, their diet would be very important. Whole groves of Araucaria trees and redwoods would have to be planted to feed a sauropod family. Entertainment value aside, these plant-eaters could be farmed as our main source of food. Maybe traditional livestock, such as

cows, sheep, and pigs, would be classed as wild animals and rarely seen, like deer today.

FUELLED ON GRASS

We have found the remains of grasses in fossil sauropod dung, so we know that they did eat grass sometimes. But this greenery wasn't a major part of the dinosaur diet because there was very little of it around at the time. If dinosaurs could evolve to eat this abundant plant, they could be as plentiful today as they were millions of years ago. However, they would have to develop the strong teeth and complex stomach of modern grass-eating animals to digest it.

TRICERATOPS

BEASTS OF BURDEN

The other main group of plant-eating dinosaurs were the ornithischian group. These consisted of two-footed ornithopods, plated stegosaurs, armored ankylosaurs, and horned ceratopsians. They had a beak at the front of the mouth, used for gathering food, and specialized teeth at the back for crushing or chopping. They ate a wider variety of plants, which could mean that ornithischians would be much more successful than the sauropods. The bigger animals might even be used as beasts of burden today. Just imagine – you could hitch a ride in a wagon... pulled by a Triceratops!

Tough stuff
Modern grasses are difficult to digest – which is why cows have two stomachs. Dinosaurs couldn't stomach it.

A TYRANT ATTACKS

Wild cattle were grazing
peacefully on the open
plains... until one animal
sensed danger and snorted
a warning. Now the herd
stampedes in terror!
A mighty Tyrannosaurus
is bearing down on them,
its enormous jaws
gaping wide!

TYRANNOSAURUS

NAME
Tyrannosaurus (say "teh-ran-no-saw-rus") means "tyrant lizard."

CLASSIFICATION
Belonged to the group of tyrannosaurid dinosaurs – amongst the last of the meat-eating theropods.

TIME
Late Cretaceous period, 67–65.5 million years ago.

HABITAT
Forest or flood plain.

FOSSIL FINDS
Montana, South Dakota, Wyoming, Colorado, and Texas; Alberta, Canada. About 20 specimens found in total.

Scary Skull

Tyrannosaurus's mouth could hold a whole cow! Its powerful jaws and teeth could bite through the thick skin and bones of a dinosaur, such as Triceratops, in one go!

SCARY SCAVENGERS

An urban fox finds a tasty treat in an overturned garbage can,
but something's got there first – a pack of Coelophysis!
These nimble dinos are scavenging, and they won't give up easily!

COELOPHYSIS

NAME
Coelophysis (say "see-low-fie-sis") means "hollow form."

CLASSIFICATION
An early theropod dinosaur.

TIME
Late Triassic period, 216.5–203.6 million years ago.

HABITAT
Arid landscapes – rocky deserts and oases.

FOSSIL FINDS
Complete skeletons found in New Mexico and Arizona.

Pack Attack

Coelophysis hunted in packs, like wolves do today. Although Coelophysis look scrawny, they were more than twice as long as wolves, and very nimble and nippy - wolves beware!

Wolf   Adult Coelophysis

RIVER RIVAL

In the cold rapids of North America, grizzly bears look on helplessly as their favorite prey - wild salmon - is hooked, and then snapped up by the claws and jaws of a Baryonyx! The bears have to wait while the dinosaur feasts on fish flesh.

BARYONYX

NAME
Baryonyx (say "bah-ree-on-icks") means "heavy claw."

CLASSIFICATION
This strange, fierce fisherman of a dinosaur is in a class of its own.

TIME
Early Cretaceous period, 130–125 million years ago.

HABITAT
Fishing along riverbanks and in lowland lakes.

FOSSIL FINDS
Complete skeleton found in England, and fragments from Niger, Africa, Spain, and Portugal.

Big Claw Clue

The first part of a *Baryonyx* skeleton ever found was an enormous claw – sticking out of a clay pit! The dino might have used its claws to hook fish out of the water, the same way grizzly bears do today.

PACK OF PESTS

A pair of fast Troodon nip and slash at the legs of a kangaroo as it bounds across the outback. Troodon's vicious claws, knife-sharp teeth, and equally sharp brain are more than a nuisance – they're lethal!

TROODON

NAME
Troodon (say "troo-don") means "wounding tooth." Ouch!

CLASSIFICATION
Belonged to the troodontid family of meat-eating theropod dinosaurs.

TIME
Late Cretaceous period, 75–65.5 million years ago.

HABITAT
Open plains.

FOSSIL FINDS

Fragments of bones and teeth from Montana, Wyoming, New Mexico, and Alaska; more complete skeleton found in Alberta, Canada.

Big Brain

In comparison to the size of its body, *Troodon* had the largest brain of all the dinosaurs. Although it was just a bit smaller than the emu of today, its brain was much larger.

Emu   Troodon

SUPERFAST DINO DERBY

Attracted by the galloping racehorses, a flock of Struthiomimus have joined in the sprint, causing chaos. They are faster than thoroughbreds – if only you could get a saddle on them!

STRUTHIOMIMUS

NAME
Struthiomimus (say "strew-thee-oh-mee-mus") means "ostrich mimic."

CLASSIFICATION
These big-eyed, long-legged dinosaurs belonged to the "bird-mimic" group of dinosaurs, the ornithomimids ("or-nith-oh-mee-mids").

TIME
Late Cretaceous period, 75–65.5 million years ago.

HABITAT
Open plains.

FOSSIL FINDS
Many complete skeletons from Alberta, Canada.

Speediest Sprinter
Struthiomimus may have been the fastest dinosaur ever. Compared to many of today's animals, including humans and racehorses, *Struthiomimus* is in the lead by a very long neck!

GREEDY BEAKS

Squawk! Oviraptor's harsh cry rings out in the quiet morning on Christmas Island. It's the red crabs' annual migration and millions of them are heading down to the sea. For Oviraptor, Christmas has come early!

TEMPORARY REQUEST
DUE TO MIGRATING CRABS

Australian
Nature
Conservation
Agency

SHIRE OF CHRISTMAS ISLAND

WOULD ALL MOTORISTS

PLEASE FOLLOW THE

RECOMMENDATION BELOW

AVOID USING THIS
ROAD IF POSSIBLE

OVIRAPTOR

NAME
Oviraptor (say "oh-vee-rap-tor")
means "egg thief."

CLASSIFICATION
Belonged to the oviraptorids – a birdlike
family of theropod dinosaurs.

TIME
Late Cretaceous period,
75 million years ago.

HABITAT
Rocky deserts and Mongolian plains.

FOSSIL FINDS
The first *Oviraptor*
was found on
top of a pile of
Protoceratops eggs
(which is how it got
its name) in Mongolia, Asia.

Freaky Beaky Ancestor?
Oviraptor has several
features like those of
today's birds – a
cassowary (shown
here), for example – and
it may have displayed its
tail feathers much the
same way a peacock does.

Cassowary

LIONS DEVOUR DINO

Ignoring its anguished cries, a pride of lionesses take down a monster Ceratosaurus. A dinosaur of this size is normally too powerful for even such a strong hunter, but old or sickly beasts become slow and weak... and, finally, dinner.

CERATOSAURUS

NAME
Ceratosaurus (say "ser-rat-toe-saw-rus") means "horned lizard."

CLASSIFICATION
This large, predatory ceratosaurian dinosaur lived alongside famous meat-eaters, such as *Allosaurus*.

TIME
Late Jurassic period, 153–148 million years ago.

HABITAT
Riversides, woodlands, and plains.

FOSSIL FINDS
Large specimens found in Utah and Colorado, as well as Portugal.

Massive Meat Menu!
Ceratosaurus had the most varied diet of any dinosaur. Everything from fish to crocodiles and antelope would be on its menu!

Ceratosaurus - meat mad!

Crocodile - on the menu?

GIGANTIC HUNTER

Lazy hippos are suddenly dwarfed by a meat-eating monster rising out of the water – Spinosaurus – the largest carnivore ever to walk the Earth! Although its diet is mainly (huge) fish, it's more than a match for a hippo... though it might be biting off more than it can chew by tackling a whole pod of them!

SPINOSAURUS

NAME
Spinosaurus (say "spine-oh-saw-rus") means "spine lizard."

CLASSIFICATION
The spinosaurs formed their own family of meat-eating theropod dinosaurs.

TIME
Early Cretaceous period, 112–97 million years ago.

HABITAT
Tidal flats, river deltas, and along the banks of North African rivers.

FOSSIL FINDS
Six fragmented specimens from Egypt, Morocco, Tunisia, Algeria, and Niger.

Croclike Shock

Spinosaurus, a colossal killer, had a long snout with sharp, smoothly pointed teeth, similar in shape to those of a crocodile. This is why scientists believe that its diet was big fish, but it may have snapped up any beast at the water's edge – again, in much the same way that crocs do today.

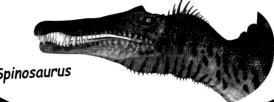

Spinosaurus

KILLERS – OR THRILLERS?

TYRANNOSAURUS

What would our world be like if large meat-eating dinosaurs roamed the planet today?

Big meal worry

One *Sauroposeidon* would feed a family of tyrannosaurs for a month. If they dined on zebras, they'd have to scoff dozens each time!

SAUROPOSEIDON

Packs of predatory meat-eating dinosaurs would be lethal if they lived in the modern world. The largest ones, such as Tyrannosaurus, might stick to their traditional prey – duckbill and long-necked sauropod dinosaurs – and ignore our smaller creatures. However, if they were quick enough to catch modern mammals, such as zebras, they might kill thousands of them! If dinosaurs had evolved alongside mammals, their digestive systems would be well adapted to this kind of food, so a snack of some cattle would keep them going.

KILLER GANGS

Medium-sized meat-eaters would be an even bigger problem. Prowling packs of Ceratosaurus would make mincemeat

SPINOSAURUS

of a herd of sheep or goats! Herders would need more than just dogs to keep these predators away.

worse; some dinosaurs might have been venomous. Imagine the terror of getting a toxic dinosaur bite!

FUN AND FIERCE

Maybe some carnivorous (meat-eating) dinosaurs could be useful - and even entertaining! Struthiomimus might be bred for racing. What could be more fun than seeing superfast dinosaurs on a racecourse? And Velociraptor would make a great and terrifying guard dog. "BEWARE OF THE DINO!"

TERROR IN THE CITY

Small meat-eaters would be the worst. They might infest our cities, scavenging for garbage, threatening our dogs and cats, and breaking into buildings and cars. Terrors such as Troodon or Coelophysis might have to be controlled like rats or other vermin. And it could be even

Reptile arena?
Imagine Spinosaurus in gladiatorial contests in ancient Rome. Quite a challenge for any gladiator!

Dino defenses
Houses would have to be more like castles if meat-eating dinosaurs still prowled around the Earth!

47

GIANT OF THE DEEP

Streaking through the ocean, Shonisaurus rushes towards its prey like a supershark going in for the kill. Its sharp eyes have caught sight of a giant octopus. With one snap of the fish-reptile's jaws, the octopus is devoured!

SHONISAURUS

NAME

Shonisaurus (say "shon-knee-saw-rus")
means "lizard of the Shoshone Mountains."

CLASSIFICATION

This very large marine reptile belonged
to the group of ichthyosaurs ("ick-thee-oh-
sawrs"), or "fish-lizards."

TIME

Late Triassic period,
215 million years ago.

HABITAT

The deep ocean; open water.

FOSSIL FINDS

Nevada; British
Columbia, Canada.

Massive Sea Monster

A *Shonisaurus* fossil skeleton found in
1998 was so big that the dino scientists
had to go up in an aircraft to see all of it!

EARTH'S LARGEST KILLER

It's behind you! A killer whale snatches a sea lion, unaware that's it about to be snatched up by even bigger jaws itself! Liopleurodon, the largest hunter ever, explodes out of the sea as it goes in for the kill.

LIOPLEURODON

NAME

Liopleurodon (say "lie-oh-plew-roh-don")
means "smooth-sided tooth."

CLASSIFICATION

Belonged to the pliosaur family of
marine reptiles, and were related to the
long-necked plesiosaurs.

TIME

Late Jurassic period,
162–150 million years ago.

HABITAT

Shallow tropical seas that covered most
of northern Europe.

FOSSIL FINDS

Huge teeth first
found in France,
but more complete
skeletons found
in Britain, France,
Germany, and Russia.

Scent of a Kill

Amazingly, *Liopleurodon* could smell
its prey miles away in the water!
It swam with its mouth open,
letting water pass through
special openings in the
roof of its mouth and
out of its nostrils.

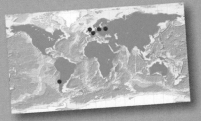

PREHISTORIC SEASHELLS

A sea otter prepares to tuck into a tasty treat, but can this modern mammal come to grips with an ancient coiled creature? Ammonites were like squids with a protective hard spiral shell – not so good to munch!

AMMONITE

NAME

Ammonite (say "am-on-ite") – after the Egyptian god Ammon, who had a pair of curled ram's horns.

CLASSIFICATION

These types of molluscs belonged to the cephalopod ("sef-a-low-pod") group, which includes modern squids, octopuses, and cuttlefish.

TIME

Devonian–Cretaceous periods, 400–65.5 million years ago.

HABITAT

Open water, spread throughout all oceans worldwide.

FOSSIL FINDS

Ammonites are found everywhere in the world.

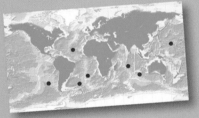

Clever Coils

Ammonites are extinct today, but during the age of the dinosaurs, the seas were full of them. They had hollow chambers in their coiled shells, which they could fill with air to rise in the water.

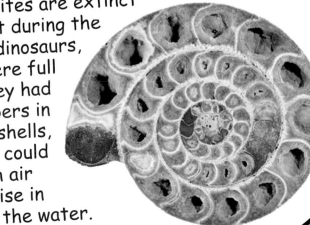

CAUGHT UP

It's an unexpected catch for these fishermen. As they haul in their net, they find that they have bagged a fearsome Mosasaurus along with their shellfish. The angry ammonite-hunter struggles and snaps its huge jaws, tearing the net to shreds!

MOSASAURUS

NAME
Mosasaurus (say "mo-za-saw-rus")
means "lizard of the Meuse River."

CLASSIFICATION
Belonged to the mosasaur family of large
swimming reptiles, closely related to modern
monitor lizards.

TIME
Late Cretaceous period,
70–65.5 million years ago.

HABITAT
Hunted in shallow waters near the ocean
surface.

FOSSIL FINDS
Many complete
skeletons from the
Netherlands; but
also Canada, the US,
and worldwide.

Big Reptile Relative
Mosasaurus is a relative of the Komodo dragon
of today - but is so much bigger, it's
mind-boggling!

Mosasaurus

Komodo dragon

CHILLING OUT

Sea lions and Cryptoclidus sun themselves on a marina. The long-necked marine reptiles have learned from the mammals that this is the place for fishy scraps and treats from tourists.

CRYPTOCLIDUS

NAME
Cryptoclidus (say "crip-toe-cl-eye-dus") means "hidden collar bone."

CLASSIFICATION
Belonged to the group of long-necked marine reptiles called the plesiosaurs.

TIME
Middle Jurassic period, 165–161 million years ago.

HABITAT
Surface waters, swimming like a seal.

FOSSIL FINDS
England, France, Russia, and South America.

Sneaky Snakey Neck

Cryptoclocidus's small head and long neck might have helped it to sneak up on squid and fish. The long neck kept its big body out of the sight of its prey – until it was too late for them to realize they were dinner!

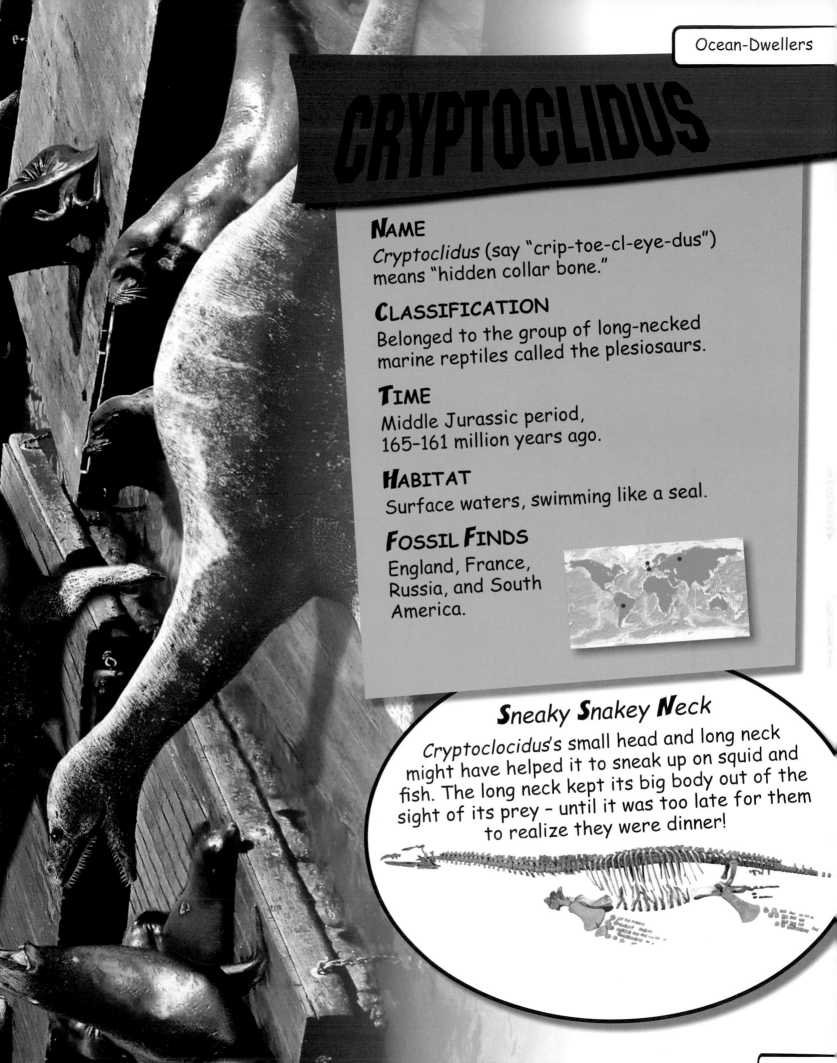

AMMONITE

Ammonite 'n' fries? These shellfish could be harvested as food for humans.

DANGER! BEACH CLOSED. PLIOSAURS SIGHTED!

Maybe they'd be in more danger from us. These sea-going creatures evolved from land animals, so some of them needed to come ashore to lay eggs. Perhaps some beaches could be designated plesiosaur nesting sites and be protected? In this case, the reptiles might still be in danger from egg-stealing poachers.

GREEN TURTLE

Would our beaches have signs like this? Or would these creatures have been hunted to the brink of extinction? Swimming meat-eaters with fierce teeth would be a worry for swimmers, but perhaps the danger wouldn't be that great – after all, even shark attacks aren't very common.

PLESIOSAUR

ICHTHYOSAUR

OUT OF THE WAY!

Plesiosaurs are thought to have swum at shallow depths under the waves, reaching down with their long necks to catch fish. A large-bodied plesiosaur just below the water's surface could pose a big problem for small boats, but boat motors would be just as big a threat to the reptile. Manatees in shallow Caribbean waters are often injured or killed by speedboat propellers. It is very likely that plesiosaurs would suffer the same fate.

The biggest of the sea reptiles might interfere with boats' radar navigation if they strayed into shallow waters, as sometimes happens today with blue whales.

Fisherman's friend?

Streamlined marine reptiles would be a challenge for sport fishers! Their cunning and strength would be a real test.

Manatee injury Would plesiosaurs get hurt the way manatees do today?

SCRUMMY SEAFOOD

If these ocean-living animals from the Age of the Dinosaurs were edible, then human beings would be bound to fish them for food... maybe even to extinction. Who knows - perhaps people would have to campaign to save ichthyosaurs in the same way they do for whales?

SAVE THE ICHTHYOSAUR!

EAGLE ATTACKED

These arrogant, early birds are harassing a mighty bald eagle, trying to get it to drop the lizard it's caught. This king of the skies is going to have a tough time avoiding these pesky Archaeopteryx!

ARCHAEOPTERYX

NAME
Archaeopteryx (say "ark-ee-op-ter-icks") means "ancient wing."

CLASSIFICATION
This small dinosaur was one of the world's first birds.

TIME
Late Jurassic period, 150.8-148.8 million years ago.

HABITAT
Along the shores of warm tropical islands.

FOSSIL FINDS
All fossils of Archaeopteryx come from Solnhofen, Germany.

Mistaken Dino Identity

For years, one fossil of Archaeopteryx was thought to be a dinosaur. It was an easy mistake to make – the sharp teeth, claws, and bony tail are totally dinolike. But it is also bird-sized and light, and has broad, feathered wings, ready to fly! This is why we know that birds evolved from dinosaurs.

HIGH-FLYING HAZARDS

A pair of Quetzalcoatlus parents make life difficult for a pilot. The massive-winged reptiles may think the plane is another beast trying to attack their nest – or maybe they're just enjoying the aerial acrobatics!

QUETZALCOATLUS

NAME
Quetzalcoatlus (say "kwet-zal-koh-at-lus"); named after the Aztec feathered-serpent god Quetzalcoatl.

CLASSIFICATION
One of the largest flying animals ever, Quetzalcoatlus belonged to the pterosaur ("terr-oh-sawr") group of flying reptiles.

TIME
Late Cretaceous period, 68–65.5 million years ago.

HABITAT
The skies over open plains.

FOSSIL FINDS
Texas.

Kings of Wings

Quetzalcoatlus had wings that were between 36 and 56 feet (11 and 17 meters) from tip to tip.
It would make an albatross (the bird with the largest wingspan) look like a sparrow!

Albatross

Quetzalcoatlus

TERRITORIAL TERRORS

A small bird flies off in fright as two aggressive Anurognathus swoop in on a garden bird feeder. They don't even eat seeds – these insect-chasing reptiles are just protecting their patch!

ANUROGNATHUS

NAME
Anurognathus (say "an-yoor-oh-nay-thuss") means "jaws with no tail."

CLASSIFICATION
This small pterosaur ("terr-oh-sawr") belonged to its own family of flying reptiles.

TIME
Late Jurassic period, 150 million years ago.

HABITAT
Forests on the shores of shallow tropical lagoons.

FOSSIL FINDS
Well-preserved fossil skeletons found in Solnhofen, Germany.

Telltale Teeth

Just as the different shapes of birds' beaks tell us a lot about what they eat, so do *Anurognathus's* small spiky teeth tell us about their diet. A big mouth lined with spikes was ideal for catching insects while *Anurognathus* was in flight. Snap! How's that for an in-flight meal?

Stork - spears fish

Hornbill - eats figs

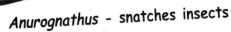
Anurognathus - snatches insects

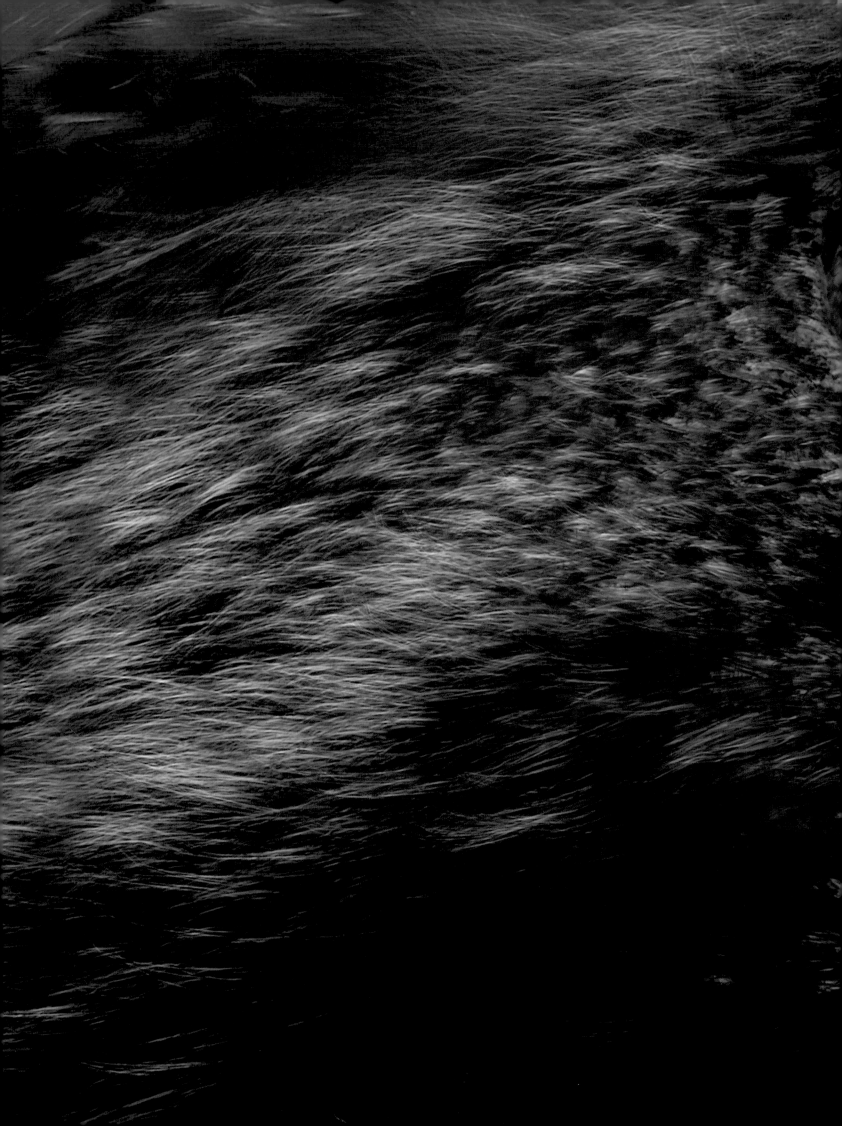

RAPTORS ON LADY LIBERTY!

Has the Statue of Liberty's face got blotches? No, they're actually Microraptors, using their long sharp claws to cling to the smooth surface.

MICRORAPTOR

NAME
Microraptor (say "my-krow-rap-tor") means "tiny hunter."

CLASSIFICATION
These feathered and flying dinosaurs belonged to the therapod group. *Microraptor* is the smallest-known dino.

TIME
Early Cretaceous period, 120 million years ago.

HABITAT
Forests surrounding freshwater lakes.

FOSSIL FINDS
More than 300 fossil specimens, mostly from Liaoning, China.

Tiny Glider

Scientists once thought that pint-sized *Compsognathus* was the smallest dino ever. That was before a fossil of tiny *Microraptor* was found. This dino was so light it could glide from tree to tree.

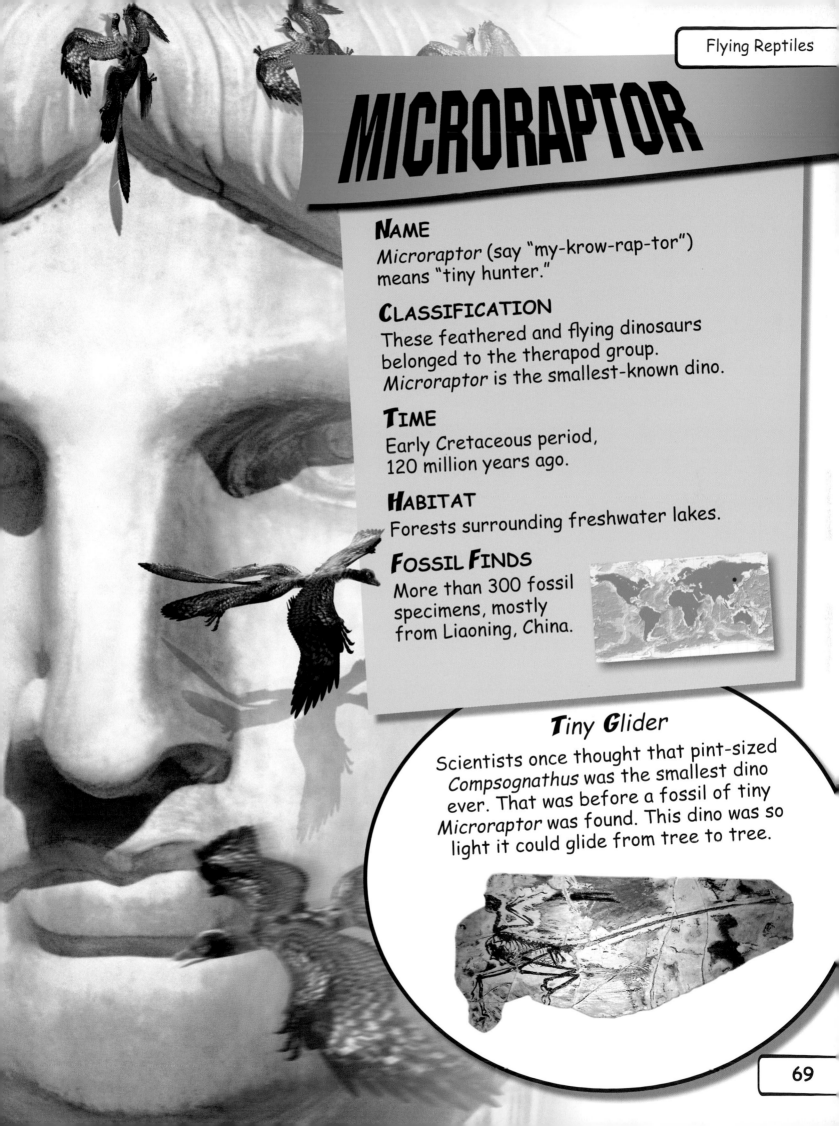

EXCITING SIGHTS — OR FLYING PESTS?

Flying reptiles would be a beautiful sight, but they could cause havoc!

Colorful crests
Pterosaurs' bright colors would rival even the most dazzling plumage of modern birds.

Imagine if the skies were full of pterosaurs as well as birds. Their bright, flashy colors would look amazing. But think of the mess! These creatures would be every bit as sneaky and cocky as any other flying animal. Spiky-toothed reptiles would hunt for fish, while those with shell-cracking jaws would poke about in rock pools. Flying fruit-eaters would descend in large noisy flocks and clear out entire orchards and farms!

THREAT FROM ABOVE

The largest flying reptiles had wingspans as big as small airplanes. These monsters could prove to be a hazard and a major worry for pilots. Although we don't know much about the lifestyles of these big pterosaurs, one thing is for sure – they certainly wouldn't be swooping down to carry off people, like they do in the movies! Pets are a different

matter, though; they might well fly off with Fido!

HIGH LIFE

Birds and flying reptiles once lived together, but pterosaurs died out at the end of the Cretaceous period. Could they share the skies again, or would the smart and talented birds make life difficult for the reptiles? Pterosaurs might struggle to cope and compete with intelligent birds that are good at taking opportunities. Pterosaurs could also struggle to get airborne in today's skies if the air had a significantly different composition. However, pterosaur young hatched fully formed and ready

ARCHAEOPTERYX

for flight. Unlike birds, they could look after themselves as soon as they were out of the egg. Birds hatch very immature young and must spend a lot of time and energy looking after them, feeding them, and preparing them for adult life. This could be an advantage for the ancient creatures.

PESTS ON WINGS

Today, we combat nuisance birds with scarecrows, bird scarers, and protective nets. These would probably be effective against pterosaurs as well, but the nets would have to be much, much stronger!

Ready to rumble
These leathery-shelled crocodile eggs are very similar to pterosaur eggs. Flying reptiles were ready to fly when they hatched.

THE END OF THE DINOSAURS

For 160 million years, dinosaurs ruled the Earth. Meat-eaters and plant-eaters evolved and lived on every continent. Their close relatives, the pterosaurs, took to the skies, and the oceans were full of giant creatures. Then... they were all gone.

Scientists don't know whether the extinction of dinosaurs happened overnight or over many thousands of years. It's difficult to know - all we have as clues are fossils, which can't be dated accurately enough to tell the full story. The other big puzzle is – why did it happen? Here are the two main theories...

SLOW DEATH

If dinosaurs dwindled away slowly, they might have been killed off by climate change or disease. A change in global temperatures might have caused new kinds of plants to grow and others to die. Plant-eating dinosaurs might not have been able to digest the new greens – so they starved to death, which meant no food for meat-eaters, so they died too.

THEORY 1

BOOM, THEN DOOM

If dinos disappeared quickly, there must have been some great disaster – perhaps a massive volcanic eruption or earthquake – or... perhaps Earth was struck by an enormous meteorite.

This last idea – that the Earth was battered by a gigantic meteorite – is now considered the most likely cause. If a huge mass of rock had crashed into the planet, the shock waves would have wiped out everything for hundreds of miles around.

The impact would have sent a huge cloud of dust into the atmosphere, and this would have blocked out sunlight for months or even years... so the plants perished, leaving plant-eating dinosaurs without food; without plant-eaters to eat, meat-eaters died out too. By the time the skies cleared, it was too late – the great dinosaurs had died out.

THEORY 2

The Chicxulub Crater

Sixty-five million years ago, a massive meteorite plunged into Earth's atmosphere. It created a vast crater on the Yucatán Peninsula of Mexico, but no sign remains on the surface today.

Chicxulub Crater

Yucatán Peninsula

MEXICO

Gulf of Mexico

Chicxulub impact material

The Mexican meteorite impact pulverized the Earth's crust. The explosion shattered rock, and tsunamis tore up the seabeds and redeposited them on land. Today, the jumbled mass of rocks on the peninsula reveals this disaster.

THE EVIDENCE

METEORITE FIND

Amazingly, there *is* evidence that a meteorite struck Earth about 65 million years ago – around the same time the dinosaurs died out.

When scientists looked at the rocks in the Earth's surface from this time, they found minerals common in meteorites. These must have fallen as dust after a huge meteorite smashed into our planet. And scientists even think they know where. In the Yucatán Peninsula in Mexico, there is a huge buried crater called Chicxulub. So here's what must have happened...

A gigantic meteorite struck the Earth, creating huge waves that smashed over North and South America. The heat from the meteorite caused massive forest

fires. A dust cloud spread across the world. Together, these aftereffects killed off the dinosaurs and all the other spectacular reptiles of the time.

LAYERS OF TIME

| | CENOZOIC ERA | 1.75 | QUATERNARY |
| | | 65 | TERTIARY |

MESOZOIC ERA
145 CRETACEOUS
200 JURASSIC
251 TRIASSIC

PALEOZOIC ERA
295 PERMIAN
355 CARBONIFEROUS
410 DEVONIAN
435 SILURIAN
500 ORDOVICIAN
540 CAMBRIAN

3.4 BILLION YEARS AGO
Our first evidence of life
is from this time.

PRECAMBRIAN

We know about the animal life that existed in times past by studying the rocks in which fossils are found. Scientists can read the rock layers like a book, telling us what the landscape and conditions were like all those years ago.

TIME

Geological history covers a stretch of time so immense that we can hardly imagine it. We are talking about thousands of millions of years! To make it easy, scientists don't think in terms of numbers of years. They divide Earth's history up into manageable chunks called "eras" and "periods."

The Age of Dinosaurs is called the Mesozoic era. (It's divided into the Triassic, Jurassic, and Cretaceous periods.) This stretch of time began 251 million years ago and ended 65 million years ago. Dinosaurs appeared at the end of the Triassic period and ruled the Earth for 160 million years – and that's about 640 times as long as humans have been around!

ERA

4 BILLION YEARS AGO
Earth's crust begins to form.

PERIOD

READING ROCKS

Our knowledge of dinosaurs comes from the fossils we find in sedimentary rocks (rocks formed from sand and mud). Sedimentary rocks are often layered. The layers are called "beds" or "strata," and they usually occur in sequences. The science of reading the layers and working out their history is called "stratigraphy."

Look at the layers shown here. Like the timeline on the left, the oldest is at the bottom and the most recently made at the top. The sandstone layer might have once been a sandbank at the mouth of a river. The layer of limestone above is made of mud from the bottom of the sea – which tells us that the sea flooded the river mouth, covering the sandbank. Above this is a layer of shale, made of silty mud, which shows where mud from a river flowed in. (However, sequences in rocks can be tricky to read because they are rarely complete and are often broken.)

USEFUL FOSSILS

Fossils found in the rocks tell the real story. Different animals lived in different time periods, so we can often use fossils to tell the age of rocks. Also, since animals lived in different environments, we can use fossils to tell the difference between, for example, a shale that formed from a muddy riverbed and one that formed from a muddy seabed. Freshwater snails won't be found in a marine shale! These clues help us to understand the world in which dinosaurs lived.

SEDIMENTARY ROCK SEQUENCE

COAL
frequently contains fossilized tree stumps.

SHALE
is made up of mud particles.

LIMESTONE
contains many fossils, including ones like this crinoid.

SANDSTONE
contains many fossils – like this footprint.

PREHISTORIC PUZZLES

DROMAEOSAURUS

How do we know what the big dinosaurs were like? By examining a few fossilized bones - or, just maybe, piecing together whole fossilized skeletons. Both involve real skill, great knowledge, and quite a bit of luck.

RARE FINDS

Our knowledge of dinosaurs is very patchy; we know a lot about some species and just a little about others. This is because it's very unusual to find a complete fossilized skeleton. Usually, all that are found are scraps and bits that must be pieced together by the experts.

SEA-LIVING ANIMALS

Most fossils are of marine animals. Why? We find fossils in sedimentary rocks, remember – and these are usually formed from mud and sand laid down under water. Sea animals are more likely to be buried in the seabed and become fossils when the sediments eventually turn to rock.

LAND-LIVING ANIMALS

A land animal rarely fossilizes. Any animal that dies on land gets torn apart by scavengers, and then eaten by maggots and insects. Bones and other hard parts are broken down by bacteria and weather, and rot away until there's nothing left.

If an animal's dead body is going to become a fossil, it has to be buried quickly in sediments. These must be covered by more sediments. If they are going to turn into rock, they have to be covered by many layers and compressed... then these rocks have to be brought to the surface and worn away until the fossils are exposed. It's no wonder that complete fossils of land animals are so rare!

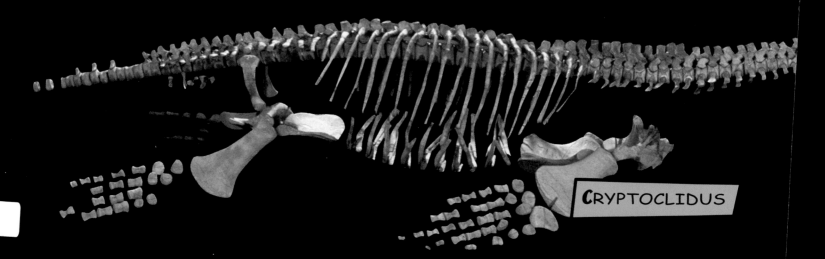

CRYPTOCLIDUS

ARTICULATED SKELETON

An articulated skeleton is one in which the bones are still joined together, as they were in life. It shows us right away what the original animal looked like. For an articulated fossil to form, a dino's dead body must be buried very quickly – before it's damaged by the elements.

ASSOCIATED SKELETON

More common is what is called an associated skeleton. This is a mixed-up jumble of bones that came from the same animal. It takes an expert to put the bones back together.

FOSSIL BONES

Usually we find isolated fossil bones. Sometimes we can tell what kind of dinosaur left that bone. Often, though, we can tell only that it is a dino bone.

TUPUXUARA

The least useful dinosaur fossils are what scientists call "float." These are scattered, weathered bones found on the surface. Luckily, even an isolated tooth or limb bone may be identified as a particular species.

Whatever its condition, a dinosaur fossil usually only contains traces of the original bone mineral (calcium phosphate). It has been in the rocks for so long that it has changed. Groundwater seeps into the bone and deposits minerals in it, usually replacing the spaces that made up the blood vessels and fat.

This is why many of the dinosaur bones we see in museums are not the white of fresh bone but the brown, black, or purple of the minerals that have replaced it.

GASOSAURUS

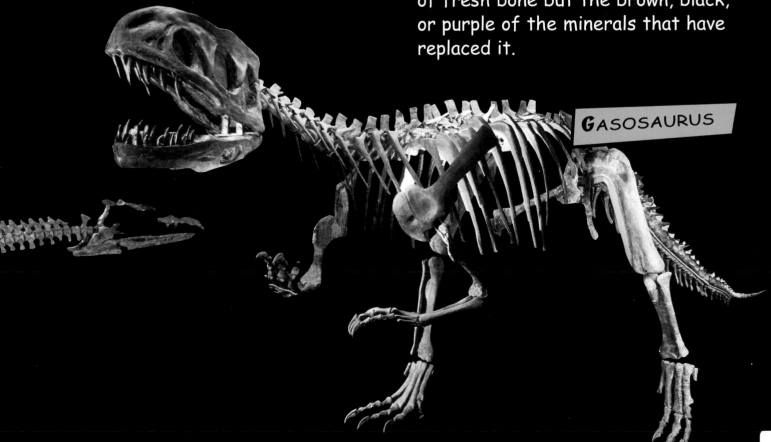

DINOSAUR DISCOVERY

Since the first dinosaur remains were identified, in England in the 1820s, dinosaur fossils have been found all over the world. Although dinosaur hunters use computers and satellites to find bones today, nothing beats a sharp eye!

Where?

19th Century The most important early dinosaur discoveries were made in the US, in the last half of the 19th century. As settlers moved west, scientists followed them and started finding skeletons. They became so jealous of each other's discoveries that they competed fiercely to unearth the most and the best skeletons. These "Bone Wars" resulted in about 150 different types of dinosaur being discovered by 1900.

20th Century People started to actively look for dinosaur fossils all over the world. German and British teams found them in

Africa; expeditions from the US discovered important remains in the Gobi Desert in Mongolia; and sheep farmers turned them up in Australia. In the 1970s, dinosaur fossils were even found in the wilderness of Antarctica.

21st Century Today, sites are being revisited and studied using modern techniques. Even greater discoveries are now being made, including dinosaurs with fossilized soft parts. More careful excavation is revealing details like stomach contents that rougher methods overlooked. Much more attention is also being paid to fossils that tell us how ancient animals lived.

MONTANA, 1897
The classic Late Cretaceous dino site.

AFRICA, 1984
Sir David Attenborough with sauropod bones.

ENGLAND, 2004
Fossilized footprint thought to belong to an *Iguanodon*.

How?

Most dinosaur discoveries are accidents. Scientists trying to find bones are faced with a difficult task. They must first locate rocks that date back to dinosaur times and that are from environments in which dinosaurs lived. Over millions of years, rocks have moved around the planet and climates have changed, so a prehistoric riverside rock might today be found in a dry desert.

Added to this is the difficulty of searching vast open spaces, such as the Gobi Desert in Mongolia. There are many tools to help dinosaur hunters, such as satellite photography. Different rocks reflect light in different ways, and scientists may recognize potentially fossil-bearing rocks from the air. With this technique, scientists can focus their ground search.

Dinosaur hunters also use radar technology to look inside rocks, see what is buried below the surface, and plan an excavation.

SATELLITE IMAGE
The Gobi Desert.

GROUND-PENETRATING RADAR
This allows scientists to see inside Earth.

Another way of finding fossils is to set off a small explosion at the surface and watch how the shock waves bounce through the rock. Bones show up because the waves travel through them differently and rebound off their edges.

Finally, sensitive instruments can detect radioactive minerals inside some fossils. However, this method has only been used in a couple of cases to date.

Could this be you?

It is hard to know where the next great dinosaur find is going to be. Currently, we know of about 500 different dinosaur types. This could represent anything from a third to a fifth of all the dinosaurs that ever lived. This means that there are many more unknown kinds of dinosaurs still in the rocks, waiting to be discovered, which will add to our knowledge of dinosaur life.

MAGNETOMETRY
These machines pick up radioactive waves from fossils.

SAICHANIA
Found in the Gobi Desert.

CHANGING PLANET

The Atlantic Ocean is 100 feet (30 meters) wider now than it was when Christopher Columbus crossed it 500 years ago! This is because Earth's continents are moving constantly, through a process called "plate tectonics."

SUPERCONTINENT

If we look at a map of the planet as it was at the beginning of the Age of Dinosaurs, we can see that all the continents are clumped together as one single landmass. This "supercontinent" - formed in the Triassic period - is called Pangaea. Dinosaurs evolved on Pangaea and spread across it. They were concentrated around the coast, because the heart of the supercontinent was a searing desert.

Fossil finds prove that the same kinds of dinosaurs lived all over the supercontinent. Modern South Africa was on the southern edge of Pangaea. Here we find the remains of long-necked plant-eating dinos, very similar to the long-necked plant-eaters we find in Germany – on the northern edge of Pangaea. Small meat-eating dinosaurs from southern and eastern Africa are similar to those in Arizona – which were the east and west sides of Pangaea.

Coelophysis
A small active theropod that hunted along North American rivers.

Plateosaurus
A prosauropod that fed on the oasis plants of Germany's dry Triassic plains.

TRIASSIC - 220 million years ago

Germany

East Africa

South Africa

Euskelosaurus
A South African prosauropod that had a similar appearance and lifestyle to *Plateosaurus* from Germany.

Syntarsus
An East African theropod that was almost identical to *Coelophysis* from North America.

Tarbosaurus
The tyrannosaurids were the big meat-eaters of the northern hemisphere.

Sauropelta
The armored dinosaurs lived mostly in North America and Asia.

CRETACEOUS – 100 million years ago

Mongolia

North America

Africa

South America

MODERN CONTINENTS

As time went on, Pangaea split up. Cracks appeared and the landmass began to drift apart. By the end of the Age of Dinosaurs, these sections had formed the modern continents and were separate from one another, and so dinosaurs that lived on these sections began to evolve in their own separate ways. By the end of the Cretaceous period, dinosaurs in North America, South America, Europe, Asia, and Africa were all completely different.

What if the dinosaurs had not become extinct 65 million years ago? They would have continued to evolve, separated by the different continents – in which case they might be very different to the ancient dinosaurs that are shown in this book.

Saltasaurus
Sauropods continued to thrive in South America but were dying out elsewhere.

Carcharodontosaurus
The big meat-eaters of the southern continents were the carnosaurs.

T. REX

CHANGING WORLD

Not only did the positions of the continents change while dinos ruled the world, climates changed too. Plant life also evolved, and all of this affected the evolution of the dinosaurs.

TRIASSIC

The first dinosaurs lived in places where water was plentiful – by the seaside, along riverbanks, and in desert oases. The vegetation was different from that found today. The undergrowth consisted mostly of horsetails, ferns, and bushy cycads. The trees were mostly conifers, of the kind that still live in the mountains of South America. Their tough spiny needles evolved to discourage the digestions of the tree-munching dinos.

Plateosaurus
The first plant-eating dinosaurs were prosauropods (pro-sawr-oh-pods) like *Plateosaurus*, with long necks, small heads, and gigantic guts!

Brachiosaurus
The long-necked sauropods of the Jurassic period could feed on both undergrowth and the tops of high trees.

JURASSIC

As climates became milder and moister in the Jurassic period, the supercontinent Pangaea began to break apart. Shallow seas flooded the continents. Forests became much more widespread and the dinosaurs flourished. New and plentiful vegetation encouraged the evolution of big plant-eating dinosaurs, and hot on their heels, monster meat-eaters...

GLEICHENITES

82

MAGNOLIA

CRETACEOUS

In the Cretaceous period, plants took a great leap in a new direction. Up to this time, plants reproduced by releasing millions of spores that were fertilized in a hit-or-miss process. Then a major new group of plants appeared – the angiosperms, or flowering plants. This new group produced fruit containing small seeds. Seeds could lie quietly until the time was right and then germinate into quick-growing plants. The new flowering plants colonized areas quickly and evolved fast. They were hugely successful and took over in many parts of the world, and the dinosaurs had to adapt to eating these new kinds of plants.

Triceratops
The narrow beaks of the Cretaceous horned dinosaurs allowed them to pick out the best bits from the new flowering plants.

MODERN

Then, after the dinos died out, the vegetation changed again. Climates became cooler and drier, and the forests began to die back. Grass, with its underground stems, was good at surviving these new conditions – and it spread everywhere.

Grass is an incredibly tough plant, and only very specialized animals like cows and horses can eat it. There were no grasslands in dinosaur times, and dinos would have been unable to digest it. This is one of the main reasons that dinosaurs would not really be able to survive today – they couldn't digest modern kinds of plants.

Today's horse – a good grazer
Modern grass-eaters have very strong teeth and complex digestive systems to eat and break down tough grass leaves.

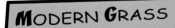

MODERN GRASS

TODAY'S DINOSAURS

Yes, dinosaurs *did* make it through the extinction event 65 million years ago – but in a completely different form. Birds evolved from meat-eating dinos in the Jurassic period, and are so closely related that you could call them "living dinosaurs."

FIRST AND FREAKIEST

The earliest bird, *Archaeopteryx*, was a strange animal. It had wings and feathers, and dinosaur features too. Instead of a beak, this bird had jaws and teeth; its wings had three clawed fingers; and it had a long bony tail – just like a dinosaur. It looks exactly as if it evolved from small meat-eating dinosaurs.

Archaeopteryx
The first bird retained many dinosaur features.

Wings
The layout of the feathers of a modern bird is just like that of *Archaeopteryx*.

Skeleton
The skeleton of a modern bird is more compact than that of its ancestor.

Tail
The fan of feathers replaces the long bony tail.

Beak
A modern bird weighs less because it has a beak instead of a toothy jaw.

Since then, birds have become the super-specialized flying animals that we know today. They have lightweight beaks and no teeth, which keeps their overall weight down. Birds' compact bodies give strong support to wing muscles, and their short, stumpy tails have a fan of feathers, to help with steering.

These days, birds look nothing like dinosaurs. Shortly after the time of *Archaeopteryx*, new and more modern-looking species of birds began to develop.

MEGABIG KILLER BIRDS

Most bird families around at the end of the Cretaceous period became extinct along with the dinosaurs. However, enough species survived to continue to present times.

Then something very strange happened. With so many plant-eating mammals around, some birds evolved into giant meat-eaters – huge flightless birds, taller than you are!

With their long hind legs, stumpy forelimbs, flexible necks, and big fierce heads, they looked a bit like their dinosaur ancestors. However, they had massive curved beaks (bigger and stronger than those of eagles), with which they killed, ripped up, and ate mammals.

There is nothing like these monster birds living now. Their places on Earth were eventually taken by meat-eating mammals like lions and wolves.

Birds continued to evolve into the animals we see today. So, perhaps you could say that dinosaurs did NOT die out. They evolved as Earth's conditions changed, and survived by growing extreme adaptations.

Dinosaurs did not become extinct – it seems they just grew wings and flew away!

Phorusrhacos
This killer bird of the early Tertiary period looked and acted just like one of the meat-eating dinosaurs it replaced.

MYTH vs FACT

BLEAK HOUSE

People have been writing stories about dinos ever since they were discovered. In his novel *Bleak House*, Charles Dickens wrote that on a murky London night you might ". . . meet a *Megalosaurus*, forty feet long or so, waddling like an elephantine lizard up Holborn Hill."

Journey to the Center of the Earth

Writers love to imagine what it would be like if dinosaurs lived today. In Jules Verne's *Journey to the Center of the Earth*, explorers venture through caves and tunnels, and find all sorts of ancient creatures. They meet up with sea reptiles like ichthyosaurs and plesiosaurs, as well as extinct mammoths.

THE LOST WORLD

The most famous fictional book about dinosaurs is *The Lost World*, by Sir Arthur Conan Doyle, the creator of Sherlock Holmes. In this book from 1912, adventurers find living dinosaurs on a plateau in South America. These dinosaurs had been isolated for millions of years while all the others had died out.

JURASSIC PARK

Using clever photography and special effects, filmmakers have brought dinosaurs to life in the movies. Perhaps the most famous dinosaur film of recent years is *Jurassic Park*. This story had scientists using traces of dinosaur blood from fossils to grow new animals. This is pure fantasy, since it would be impossible to clone extinct animals that way. However, the filmmakers consulted top scientists to help them create some amazingly lifelike dinosaurs.

Wouldn't it be great if dinosaurs really *were* alive today? Plenty of writers and artists have had fun imagining what it might be like! So, even if you can't see them in the wild, you can read books and comics, and watch films and TV programs, which vividly bring dinosaurs back to life.

STEGOCERAS

This was just ten years after the word "dinosaur" had been invented by a famous British scientist, Sir Richard Owen. At the time, people thought that dinos must have looked like gigantic lizards walking on four legs. However, by 1858 scientists realized that some walked on two legs.

By this time scientists were getting a clearer idea of what dinos looked like. Many different types had been found, including mummified duck-billed dinosaurs with preserved muscles and skin. The descriptions of *The Lost World* dinosaurs were not so different from what we understand today.

VELOCIRAPTOR

Our knowledge of what dinosaurs looked like is changing all the time!

WHAT IF... ?

Q What defines a dinosaur?

A. Their hip bones. The way these are arranged let them walk with their legs held straight under them.

Q Why is a dinosaur called a dinosaur?

A. The word Dinosauria was made up in 1842 by British scientist Sir Richard Owen – even though there were only three dinosaurs known at the time! It means "terrible lizard."

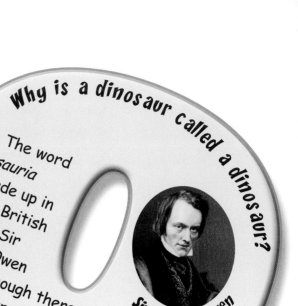

Sir Richard Owen

Q Are there any dinosaurs alive today?

Yes! Birds are so closely related to the dinos that they may as well be called "avian dinosaurs."

Q Did humans ever live alongside dinos?

No. Dinos had been dead for over 60 million years before humans evolved.

Q Could we bring dinosaurs back to life from their fossilized DNA?

No. It's unlikely that DNA (the building blocks of all creatures) could survive intact over millions of years. It makes an excellent story, however!

Q How could we look after dinosaurs today?

Well, we'd need a very big zoo! We would also need vast farms to produce enough food to feed these hungry beasts.

Q Could some dinos have survived in an unexplored part of the world?

A big dinosaur needs a huge area of land to support it. We would have discovered such a large area of land by now.

Is the Loch Ness Monster a dinosaur?

A.
Definitely not. No dinosaurs lived in the water, but if the Loch Ness Monster really exists, it could be a plesiosaur (or a relative of one). A plesiosaur was a reptile that was well adapted to life in the water, with streamlined body and head, plus paddlelike limbs.

Q Could we have kept dinosaurs as pets?
Archaeopteryx and small feathered dinos might make good pets – they would need the same sort of care as parrots.

Q If dinos had not died out 65 million years ago, would we be here?
No. Mammals were successful only because the dinosaurs died out. In the Age of Dinosaurs, all the spaces for large animals were taken by dinosaurs and other big reptiles, and mammals were small and mouselike.

When the dinos died out, suddenly there was no competition, and large plant-eating mammals were able to evolve. New meat-eating animals also evolved – first, giant flightless birds, and then carnivorous mammals.

We could not have evolved if dinosaurs were still the ruling animals.

Q Is it true that the rhinoceros descended from Triceratops?
No. These are totally different animals. They look similar because they both evolved to cope with a similar lifestyle.

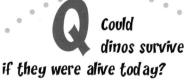

Q Could dinos survive if they were alive today?
Who knows? With the right things to eat, they probably would. Plant-eaters would find it difficult because they were fussy about what they ate.

WHAT WERE THEY REALLY LIKE?

EYES

Q **Did dinosaurs have slit eyes?**
Perhaps. If active meat-eaters hunted like modern cats, they might have had the same kind of eyes.

Q **What was dinosaur eyesight like?**
Hunting dinos would have had sharp eyesight to keep prey in view and accurately judge distances. Plant-eaters would have been better off with all-around vision.

Q **Were any dinosaurs nocturnal?** *Troodon* had large eyes – so it may have hunted at night. Small plant-eating *Leaellynasaura* lived in the Antarctic Circle, where the nights last for months. It must have been able to forage in the dark.

TEETH

Q **Which dinosaur had the most teeth?**
Duck-billed dinosaurs such as *Edmontosaurus* had literally hundreds of teeth. However, most of these were replacement teeth and were not used at the same time.

Why did different dinosaurs have different teeth?
It depended on the jobs the teeth had to do. A great meat-ripping dino, such as *Tyrannosaurus rex*, had a straight line of teeth, like a sharp saw. Plant-munching *Plateosaurus* had overlapping teeth that allowed them to grind away at the greenery – like a vegetable grater!

MALE/FEMALE

Q **How do you tell the difference between female and male dinosaurs?**
Sometimes the hip bones have different shapes. Often in fossilized dino herds we find two different sizes of adults. The females' hips are larger – because they produced eggs.

Q **Were pack leaders female or male?**
As with most of today's pack animals, the leader would have been male.

Which dino had the biggest teeth?
The biggest teeth found so far belong to *Giganotosaurus* and are about 6 inches (15 centimeters) long. This picture is life-sized!

FUNCTION

Q **What color was dinosaurs' blood?**
It would probably have contained the same chemicals as the blood of modern reptiles, and so would have the same rich red colour.

Q **How far could dinosaurs travel?**
Many big plant-eating dinos may have migrated hundreds of miles each season.

Q **How did dinosaurs fight?**
With teeth, with horns, with spikes, with tail clubs, with claws – whatever they had!

Q **Were any dinosaurs renowned for their brilliant camouflage?**
Although we don't know what color dinosaurs were, it seems likely that hunters could see in color, to pick out their prey, and plant-eaters were probably camouflaged.

Q **Would a long neck help a dinosaur?**
Yes. Like the hose of a vacuum cleaner, it would reach around without having to move its big, heavy body.

Q **What kind of skin did dinosaurs have?**
Fossilized skin is rare, but the specimens we do have show flat, joining scales. Some had bony bumps covered in horn; small meat-eating dinosaurs were covered in feathers.

BIRTH & DEATH

Q **Did dinosaurs give birth to live young or lay eggs?**
We know that plenty of dinos laid eggs. The pachycephalosaurs had wide hips, however, which suggests they may have given birth to live young.

Q **How quickly did dinosaurs grow up?**
Small meat-eaters like *Troodon* took three to five years to reach adulthood. A big sauropod like *Bothriospondylus* may have taken 43 years to become an adult.

Q **Did dinosaurs suffer from any diseases?**
Yes. We find deformities in fossil bones that were obviously caused by disease. The nodule on these bones is a tumor.

Q **Were prehistoric parasites deadly critters?**
Parasites evolved to live on a specific host, so would have been able to kill off a sickly dinosaur.

Q **How long did dinosaurs live?**
Small meat-eaters probably had short lives. Large meat-eaters such as *Tyrannosaurus* lived to about 30, while big sauropods may have lived to be over 100.

Q **What dinosaur lived the longest?**
Cold-blooded animals tend to live longer. If the big sauropods were warm-blooded, they may have lived to 120 years. If they were cold-blooded, they may have survived to 200 years.

DO YOU KNOW...?

Q *Did all dinosaurs live at the same time?* No. *Ankylosaurus*, for example, lived 75 million years after *Stegosaurus* had died out.

ANKYLOSAURUS

STEGOSAURUS

Q *What color were the dinosaurs?* Skin color never fossilizes, but we can make guesses at dino colors by comparison with modern animals. If a color scheme works for a modern animal, it would have worked just as well for any prehistoric animal in a similar environment. This is why artists paint meat-eating dinosaurs in tiger stripes and plant-eaters in dull greys, like elephants.

Q *Were dinosaurs the same all over the world?* No. At the start of the Age of Dinosaurs, there were many similar kinds of dinos living all over the supercontinent of Pangaea, but as time went on, different types evolved. When Pangaea split apart, the dinosaur types on the different continents became more unlike each other.

Q *How can we be sure that dinosaurs really look like how we show them?* That is a difficult question! Our view of what dinosaurs looked like changes all the time. Early scientists imagined that they looked like giant lizards. *Iguanodon*, for example, was drawn like a gigantic iguana. **(1)** A later discovery was that dinosaur legs did not stick out at the sides, like a lizard's, but the bones were upright and supported the body like pillars. Scientists figured that dinos looked more like mammals, which have straight legs. Imagine an *Iguanodon* that looked like a rhinoceros! **(2)** When complete skeletons were discovered for the first time, scientists could see how the animal was put together. *Iguanodon* from this period looks like a kangaroo, sitting back on its hind legs and supported by its tail. **(3)** Today, we think *Iguanodon* was a four-footed animal that walked with its tail held in the air – **(4)** – but who knows; we might find out something new that would change our ideas again.

1

2

3

4

TRICERATOPS

SPECIES

Q *What is the most common dinosaur?*
Triceratops is sometimes found in fossil beds containing over a thousand individuals. These enormous herds make this dino the most common.

Q How many species of dinosaurs were there? We know of over 500, but more are dug up every year.

Q *What came before dinos?*
Almost all the kinds of animals that we have today – fish, insects, amphibians, reptiles – except for birds. Mammals evolved at about the same time as the dinosaurs.

TYRANNOSAURUS

FIRST & LAST

Q *Which were the first and last dinosaurs on Earth?*
The earliest-known dino was *Eoraptor* – a small meat-eater from the late Triassic period in South America. It's hard to say which dino was the last, since they all died out together, but *T. rex* and *Triceratops* were living at the time.

Coelacanth

EORAPTOR

DISCOVERIES

Q *Which was the first dinosaur to be discovered?* Megalosaurus.

Q *Which place is best for fossil-finding?* The US Midwestern states, such as Montana, and parts of China.

Q *Which rocks are best for dinosaur bones?* Rocks that formed in dinosaur times, especially those made from deposits laid down in lakes, riverbeds, and deserts.

Q *What is the oldest fossil ever?* Probably three-and-a-half-billion-year-old fossilized bacteria.

Q *Will all dinosaur fossils be discovered?*
No. We can only find fossils that lie near the surface – most are buried too deep.

Q Are there any more dinosaurs yet to be found? Oh yes! Just a fraction have been discovered. There will be many more buried in remote corners of the world. Maybe you'll find one?

Glossary

Ammonite An extinct marine mollusc with a spiral shell, found as fossils in rocks that date from the Jurassic and Cretaceous periods.

Amphibian An animal that can live both on land and in water. Frogs and toads are amphibians.

Arthropod An invertebrate animal that has a shell or case and jointed limbs. Insects, spiders, and crustaceans are arthropods.

Archaeology The study of our history and the Earth's prehistory through digging up sites and examining what's found there.

Arid Dry, with little or no rain – like a desert.

Atmosphere The layer of gases that surrounds the Earth.

Avian To do with birds.

Bacteria Microscopic organisms that can cause disease.

Carnivore An animal that feeds on meat.

Cephalopod "Head-footed" animals. The octopus and squid – the cephalopods of today – look as if their legs branch from their faces.

Ceratopsian dinosaur A type of dinosaur that had frills, spikes, and horns as protection.

Coal A black rock made of crushed and carbonized plants, used as fuel.

Conifer A type of tree with cones and needle- or scale-like leaves.

Continent One of the world's main, big, continuous areas of land.

Cycad A tall, palmlike plant that can be found in tropical regions.

Duckbill A type of dinosaur that had a beak like a duck's bill.

Era A division of geological time, smaller than an eon but larger than a period. Eras last for hundreds of millions of years, and cover several "periods". The Mesozoic era, for example, was made up of the Triassic, Jurassic, and Cretaceous periods.

Erosion The gradual wearing away of rocks or soil.

Evolution The way that different kinds of living organisms develop from earlier forms.

Excavation The removal of soil and rocks.

Fauna The animals of any particular place or time.

Fern A flowerless plant that has feathery or leafy fronds.

Flora The plants of any particular place or time.

Fossil The remains or impression of a prehistoric plant or animal preserved in rock.

Geology The study of the Earth – how it was made, how it changed, and how it's still changing.

Glaciated Covered or having been covered by glaciers or ice sheets.

Herbivore An animal that eats only plants.

Horsetail A flowerless plant with a hollow, jointed stem.

Ice Age A period of time when climates were cooler than they are now and glaciers covered lots of the planet.

Ichthyosaur A group of swimming reptiles from the Mesozoic era. They had fishlike bodies and tail fins.

Invertebrate An animal that doesn't have a spine.

Landmass A continent or other large body of land.

Mass extinction The dying out of a large number of animals and plants. There have been about five mass extinctions in the history of life on Earth; there's a huge one going on now.

Membrane A thin skin or similar covering.

Meteorite A rock from space.

Mineral A naturally formed inorganic substance with a specific chemical composition. Minerals are the building bricks of rocks.

Mollusc A type of invertebrate animal, often with some kind of shell.

Mosasaur A member of a group of big swimming reptiles of the Cretaceous period, closely related to modern monitor lizards.

Nocturnal Active at night.

Oases Areas in a desert where there is water – and so plants grow.

Open plains Wide spaces without trees.

Organism An individual animal, plant, or single-celled life-form.

Ornithischian A beaked, herbivorous dinosaur that roamed in herds.

Ornithopod A kind of plant-eating dinosaur that walked on two legs and lived during the Late Triassic, Jurassic, and Cretaceous periods.

Paleo- Found at the beginning of a few long words in this book! It means "ancient."

Paleontology The study of ancient life and fossils.

Period A division of geological time that can be defined by the types of animals or plants that lived then. A period lasts for tens of millions of years.

Plankton The tiny animal and plant life that drifts in the waters of the ocean.

Plate tectonics The way the Earth's surface is always being created and destroyed. New surface is being formed at ocean ridges, while old material is being lost down ocean trenches. This movement makes the continents move over the Earth's surface.

Plateau A flat area of high land.

Plesiosaur A large marine reptile of the Mesozoic era, with large, paddlelike limbs and a long flexible neck.

Pliosaur A plesiosaur with a short neck, large head, and massive toothed jaws.

Primitive A very early stage in the development of a species.

Prosauropod Late Triassic period ancestors of long-necked, plant-eating dinosaurs.

Pterosaur One of a group of flying reptiles from the Mesozoic. They had leathery wings supported by an elongated finger. *Pterodactylus* was a pterosaur.

Pulverize To crush something into powder.

Reef A ridge on the seabed that makes the sea very shallow. Most reefs are formed from the remains of living creatures.

Rift valley A steep-sided valley formed by the Earth's surface lowering between faults.

Rock A naturally formed substance that makes up the Earth. Most rocks are made of lots of different minerals.

Sauropod A huge herbivorous dinosaur, with a long neck, long tail, small head, and trunklike legs.

Savannah A grassy plain in a hot country with few or no trees.

Scavenger An animal that feeds off prey other animals have killed.

Sediment Matter carried by water or wind and then laid on the land or seabed.

Sedimentary A type of rock that formed from sediment.

Shingle A mass of small rounded pebbles, especially on a seashore.

Silica A hard, unreactive, colorless compound that occurs as quartz, and as the principal constituent of sandstone and other rocks.

Stegosaur A herbivorous dinosaur with a double row of large bony plates along the back.

Strata Layers or series of layers of rock.

Stratigraphy The type of geology that studies strata, what they mean, and what they contain.

Tectonics Large-scale processes that affect the Earth's crust.

Theropod A carnivorous dinosaur that walked on two legs and had long jaws, three-toed hind legs, and small front legs with clawed hands.

Tissue The living substance of a body, made of cells.

Trilobite A segmented arthropod, common in Paleozoic seas.

Tsunami A long, high sea wave caused by an earthquake or other disturbance.

Tyrannosaurid A type of dinosaur with a broad, massive skull, a short, powerful neck, and reduced "arms" with only two digits.

Vertebrate An animal with a backbone.

Volcano A mountain or hill with a crater or vent out of which lava, rock fragments, hot vapor, and gas can erupt.

Index